Leonard Bernstein
Music for Two Pianos

This edition published 2006

ISBN 978-1-4234-0995-3

LEONARD
BERNSTEIN
Music Publishing
Company LLC

BOOSEY & HAWKES

AN IMAGEM COMPANY

DISTRIBUTED BY

HAL•LEONARD®
CORPORATION
7777 W. BLUEMOUND RD. P.O. BOX 13819 MILWAUKEE, WI 53213

www.leonardbernstein.com
www.boosey.com
www.halleonard.com

Music for Two Pianos

Leonard Bernstein
(1937)

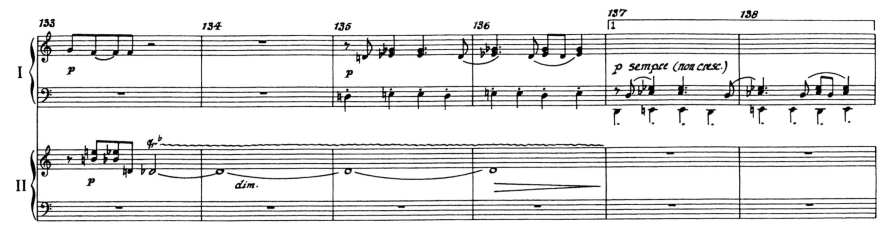

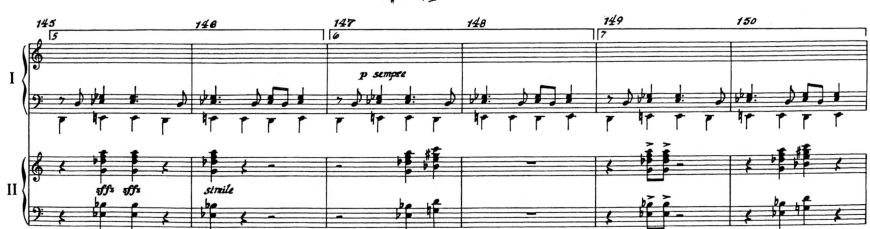

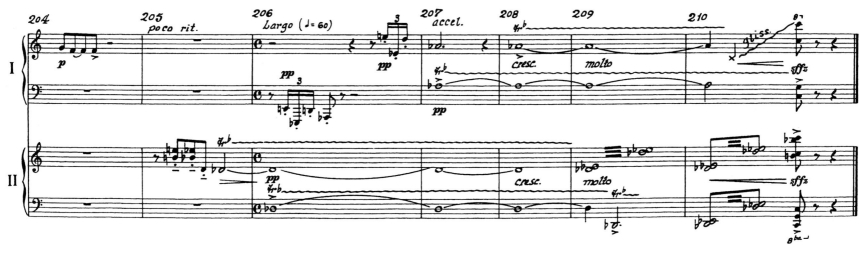